CONTENTS

HURRICANE HUNTERS

A 2005 satellite image shows Hurricane Rita almost covering the Gulf of Mexico. Rita caused havoc on the Louisiana and Texas coasts.

Tropical cyclones are large storm systems that develop over the world's warm southern oceans. Hurricanes are tropical cyclones that form in the Atlantic and North East Pacific and then travel towards the south-eastern United States.

RIDERS ON THE STORM

Hurricane hunters are paid to fly through some of the worst weather on Earth. Their mission is to gather data on the state of the storm and relay it by radio to a weather lab. They work out the direction, or track, of a storm by crisscrossing through the central eye. The winds circling the eye can rage at speeds of up to 260 kilometres per hour.

FIRST FLIGHT

It was a US Air Force colonel named Joseph Duckworth who pioneered the technique of flying through hurricanes. He flew his AT-6 Texan through the centre of the 1943 Surprise Hurricane *twice* to win a bet about the plane's strength.

An AT-6 Texan

Today's military hurricane hunters are specially equipped Hercules transports called WC-130s. They are flown by the 53rd Weather Reconnaissance Squadron out of Keesler Air Force Base in Biloxi, Mississippi, USA.

Lockheed WP-3D Orion

OBSERVE, REPORT AND STAY SAFE

Civilian hunts are undertaken by the Aircraft Operations Center of the National Oceanic and Atmospheric Administration (NOAA) based in Tampa, Florida, USA. Their largest aircraft, WP-3D Orions, are based on a tough old airliner design. Packed with equipment and their 16-member crews, the Orions tackle the most challenging missions. One of these, the launching of parachute probes at low altitude, gathers vital data on air pressure and sea surface temperature.

The eyewall of Hurricane Katrina is made up of layer upon layer of thunderstorms. Forces in the eyewall can test an aircraft to its very limits...and beyond.

Weather labs use the hurricane hunter's data to predict a storm's strength at landfall. Hurricanes destroy with their winds, and by flooding from storm surge, seen here in the aftermath of Hurricane Katrina in 2005. Early warning can aid evacuation.

TORNADO CHASERS

Tornadoes are rapidly rotating columns of air that can reach down from the bases of huge thunderstorms. Tornadoes are the most violent storms on the planet.

WHY CHASE TORNADOES?

Why is it that some supercell thunderstorms spawn tornadoes while others don't? How does tornadogenesis occur? Meteorologists need answers if they want to predict future outbreaks. Severe weather specialists chase and capture tornadoes using video, photography and radar.

Chased by a team from the US National Severe Storms Lab in 1995, the Dimmitt Tornado, in Texas, is the most thoroughly observed storm in history…so far.

Tornadoes can be killers, like this twister that struck Union City, Oklahoma, USA, in 1973. The first to have its life cycle captured on radar, the Union City tornado helped scientists develop the early warning systems we have today.

GRAPHIC CAREERS

HURRICANE HUNTERS
&TORNADO
CHASERS

by Gary Jeffrey

illustrated by Gianluca Garofalo

W

FRANKLIN WATTS
LONDON•SYDNEY

First published in 2010 by Franklin Watts

Franklin Watts
338 Euston Road
London NW1 3BH

Franklin Watts Australia
Level 17/207 Kent Street
Sydney, NSW 2000

A CIP catalogue record for this book is available from the British Library.

Dewey number: 551.5'5

ISBN: 978 0 7496 9254 4

Franklin Watts is a division of Hachette Children's Books, an Hachette UK company.
www.hachette.co.uk

GRAPHIC CAREERS: HURRICANE HUNTERS & TORNADO CHASERS
produced for Franklin Watts by David West Children's Books, 7 Princeton Court,
55 Felsham Road, London SW15 1AZ

Designed and produced by
David West Children's Books

Editor: Gail Bushnell

Photo credits:
P4t, NASA, 4m&b, U.S. Air Force photo; 5t&m, NOAA, 5b, U.S. Air Force photo by
Master Sgt. Bill Huntington; p6&7&45, all images from NOAA

Printed in China

Website disclaimer:
Note to parents and teachers: Every effort has been made by the Publishers to ensure
that the websites in this book are suitable for children, that they are of the highest
educational value, and that they contain no inappropriate or offensive material.
However, because of the nature of the Internet, it is impossible to guarantee that the
contents of these sites will not be altered. We strongly advise that Internet access is
supervised by a responsible adult.

Fewer than 20 percent of all supercells will spawn a tornado. No one knows when or where they will happen. Thousands of kilometres can be covered in fruitless search.

PATIENCE AND CAUTION

Chasers in the mid-west USA form a recognisable community. To be successful, the storm spotters, meteorologists, amateur chasers and tour operators rely on each other for information and help, especially if they get into difficulties. There are many potential hazards, from extreme winds, falling debris and lightning strikes to increased risk of car accidents.

INFORMATION GATHERING

Cell phones, laptop computers and satellite navigation are the tools of the modern chaser. Doppler trucks carry radar equipment; other vehicles have weather stations. Wireless Internet enables live feeds of the developing storm on the road.

A fleet of chase cars have roof-mounted sensors to measure wind speed and direction, air temperature and humidity.

A Doppler radar truck

A visual display from a Doppler truck shows a tornado in progress.

JEFFREY MASTERS
FLIGHT DIRECTOR
HURRICANE HUNTER 42

A NATIVE OF DETROIT, MICHIGAN, USA, JEFFREY MASTERS COMPLETED HIS MASTER'S DEGREE IN METEOROLOGY IN 1983 AND BY 1986 HAD JOINED THE NOAA AIRCRAFT OPERATIONS CENTER IN MIAMI.

IN SEPTEMBER 1989, HE FINDS HIMSELF AT GRANTLEY ADAMS FIELD IN BARBADOS, DIRECTING A LOCKHEED P3 FLIGHT, NOAA 42, INTO THE HEART OF HURRICANE HUGO...

UNITED STATES DEPT. OF COMMERCE

MY MAIN JOB IS TO OVERSEE THE SAFETY OF THE MISSION FROM A WEATHER POINT OF VIEW.

WE'LL BE GOING IN LOW, AT FIFTEEN HUNDRED FEET, TO DEPLOY SEA TEMPERATURE PROBES.

JANICE GRIFFITH IS A REPORTER COVERING THE MISSION.

BUT IF I THINK IT'S GETTING TOO DANGEROUS, I WILL CALL FOR US TO CLIMB TO A HIGHER ALTITUDE.

AIRCRAFT COMMANDER LOWELL GENZLINGER BRIEFS GRIFFITH ON SAFETY PROCEDURES...

...PULL THIS TOGGLE AND IT WILL INFLATE. A LIFE RAFT IS SITUATED OVER THERE.

AIR SICKNESS BAGS ARE STOWED HERE. OKAY?

WHERE ARE THE PARACHUTES?

ER... WE DON'T CARRY PARACHUTES.

WHERE WE'RE GOING THEY WOULDN'T DO US ANY GOOD.

FINALLY, THEY BURST INTO THE EYE, BUT...

FIRE IN ENGINE NUMBER THREE!

PLOOOOOM!

THE PILOTS RESPOND QUICKLY...

SHUTTING IT DOWN!

COMING OUT OF THE DIVE...

MASTERS CHECKS THE DAMAGE...

FIRE'S OUT IN NUMBER THREE BUT THERE'S A PIECE OF WING HANGING OFF NUMBER FOUR!

JUST PRAY IT DOESN'T FOUL THE PROPELLER...

STEVE WADE IS FLIGHT ENGINEER ON DECK.

ENGINE 4

...AND IT'S GETTING PRETTY HOT, TOO.

OIL TEMP

THE PILOTS PUT NOAA 42 INTO A SLOW SPIRALLING CLIMB...

COME ON, BABY...

BRRRAAAGH

THEY ARE TRAPPED INSIDE THE 12 KILOMETRE-WIDE EYE.

OKAY, EVERYBODY CAN BREATHE EASY. WE'RE SAFE FOR NOW.

WHAT'S THE PLAN?

WE PULLED OVER FIVE G'S IN THAT TURBULENCE. THE P-3'S ONLY RATED FOR THREE!

IF THE PLANE'S FRAME IS DAMAGED AND WE TRY TO PUNCH BACK OUT NOW, THE WALL CLOUD WILL PROBABLY RIP OUR WINGS OFF.

*G'S—SHORT FOR G-FORCE.

SO WE'RE GOING TO LIGHTEN THE AIRCRAFT BY DUMPING FUEL TO CLIMB HIGH AND BREAK OUT WHERE THERE'S LESS TURBULENCE.

AFTER THE FUEL DUMP, THEY JETTISON PARACHUTE PROBES TO LOSE MORE WEIGHT.

TEAL-57, THIS IS NOAA 42...

...WE ARE CIRCLING AT FIVE THOUSAND FEET. COULD YOU COME FLY BY AND LOOK US OVER FOR DAMAGE?

U.S. AIR FORCE

SURE THING!

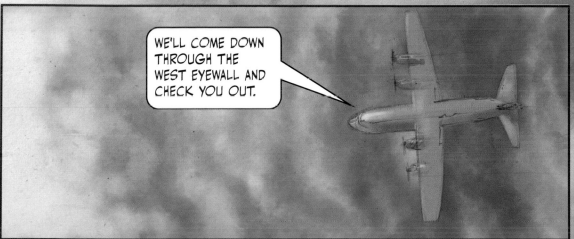

WE'LL COME DOWN THROUGH THE WEST EYEWALL AND CHECK YOU OUT.

CREW! TIME TO LOCK EVERYTHING DOWN.

FIVE MINUTES LATER...

WHOOO, THAT WAS ONE HECK OF A BUMPY RIDE!

US AIR FORCE

OTHER THAN THE PIECE OF WING, THERE'S NO OBVIOUS DAMAGE TO NUMBER FOUR ENGINE. AIRFRAME LOOKS OKAY TOO.

ROGER THAT!

AT 4,572 METRES NOAA 43 ENTERS THE EYE...

NOAA 42 WHAT IS YOUR ALTITUDE?

SEVEN THOUSAND FEET.

CAN WE GET ANY HIGHER?

NO, NUMBER FOUR IS AT ITS LIMIT.

ZZZZZT...THIS IS TEAL-57...

...WE ARE GOING THROUGH THE WEST EYEWALL TO TEST HOW ROUGH IT IS. STAND BY...

BROOOOUGH

TEAL-57, THAT IS GREATLY APPRECIATED!

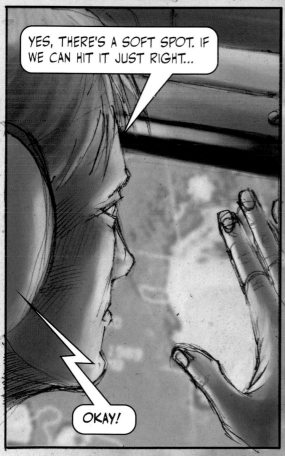

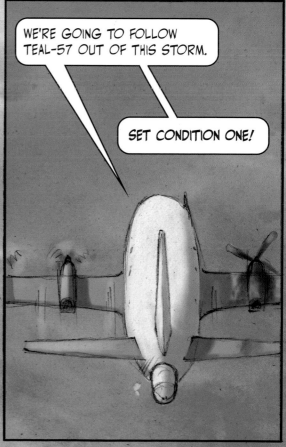

NOAA 42, THIS IS NOAA 43 WE WILL ESCORT YOU HOME.

AT LEAST I MANAGED TO SEND OFF A VORTEX REPORT*.

*INFORMATION, INCLUDING THE HURRICANE'S POSITION. HUGO GOES ON TO DEVASTATE CARIBBEAN ISLANDS AND THE CAROLINA COAST.

LATER, THEY WILL ANALYSE RADAR DATA AND DISCOVER THAT NOAA 42 WAS HIT BY A TORNADO-LIKE VORTEX EMBEDDED IN HUGO'S EYEWALL.

SUCH PHENOMENA HAVE NEVER BEEN ENCOUNTERED BEFORE. NOAA 42'S FLIGHT HAS PROVIDED VALUABLE DATA ON THE MYSTERIES OF HURRICANES.

JEFFREY MASTERS NEVER FLIES ANOTHER MISSION AND SOON LEAVES NOAA TO BECOME A REGULAR METEOROLOGIST...

...WITH HIS FEET FIRMLY ON THE GROUND!

THE END

ROGER EDWARDS
TORNADO CHASER
NATIONAL WEATHER SERVICE

AS A CHILD GROWING UP IN TEXAS, USA, ROGER EDWARDS HAD ALWAYS BEEN FASCINATED BY THE VIOLENT STORMS THAT REGULARLY BLEW IN FROM THE NORTH. THEN, ONE SUMMER'S EVENING IN 1976...

...I REPEAT, THIS IS A TORNADO WARNING FOR DALLAS COUNTY...

...A FUNNEL CLOUD HAS BEEN REPORTED IN IRVING...

...WE ADVISE ALL...

GOT TO SEE THIS!

WEEEEEEEEEEEEEARRRRRRRRR

SIREN!

THE SIGHTING GETS EDWARDS HOOKED. DURING HIS SCHOOL YEARS HE READS EVERYTHING HE CAN FIND ABOUT SUPERCELLS AND TORNADOES.

HE RESOLVES TO BECOME A SEVERE WEATHER METEOROLOGIST AND, AFTER EARNING A BACHELOR OF SCIENCE DEGREE, STARTS GAINING EXPERIENCE.

NATIONAL HURRIC... CENTER MIAMI

BY 3 MAY 1999, HE HAS SETTLED DOWN TO RAISE A FAMILY IN OKLAHOMA – WORKING THE NIGHT SHIFT AS A FORECASTER AT THE STORM PREDICTION CENTER (SPC) IN NORMAN...

YAWN...RICH, YEAH, I JUST WOKE UP.

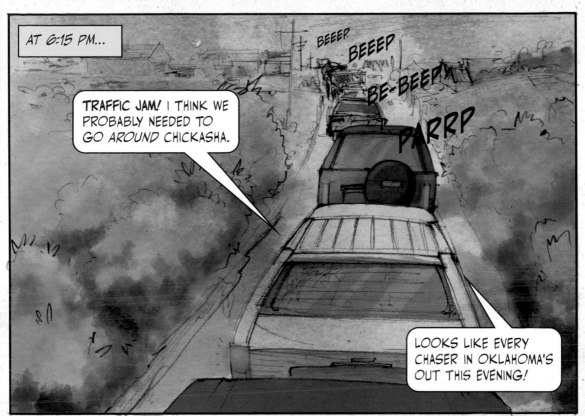

AT 6:15 PM...

TRAFFIC JAM! I THINK WE PROBABLY NEEDED TO GO AROUND CHICKASHA.

BEEEP
BEEEP
BE-BEEP
PARRP

LOOKS LIKE EVERY CHASER IN OKLAHOMA'S OUT THIS EVENING!

6:20 PM DOPPLER ON WHEELS NO 2, EIGHT KM OUT OF CHICKASHA...

WOW, LOOK AT THAT.

IT'S A CLASSIC 'HOOK ECHO'!*

*RADAR IMAGE OF A STORM'S MESOCYCLONE (SPINNING CENTRE).

THE DOPPLER TRUCK IS MANNED BY CHASER JOSH WURMAN...

RFD* MUST BE ROCKETING!

*REAR FLANK DOWNDRAFT—FAST-MOVING, DRY AIR WRAPPING AROUND THE BACK OF THE MESOCYCLONE.

TORNADO FUEL! LOOKS LIKE THERE'S A NEW ONE FORMING...

...RIGHT THERE.

NORTH-EAST OF MIDDLEBURG, 6:45 PM...

MAN, LOOK AT THE SIZE OF THAT WEDGE!

COME IN STORM CENTRE, WE'VE GOT A TORNADO ON THE GROUND HEADED FOR...

'I SURE HOPE THOSE FOLKS GOT OUT OF THERE...'

NNNNAAAAAGHWAAAAAAAA

THE DOPPLER RADAR WILL MEASURE SPEEDS ABOVE 523 KM PER HOUR, THE FASTEST WIND EVER RECORDED.

THE STORMS RAGE ON INTO THE EVENING, SPAWNING MANY MORE TORNADOES. THEN, AT 9:25 PM, IN THE CRESCENT/MULHALL AREA...

PZZZZZZZZZT

THIS ONE'S GOING TO BE A BIGGIE...

POWER LINES ARE GOING DOWN!

MUWAAAAAAARRRRGH

IT'S DIFFICULT TO SEE FROM ONE SIDE TO THE OTHER. IT'S SO BIG!

WOOOOOOO ...HA! HA!

BZZZZZT

EDWARDS IS DUE ON SHIFT AT MIDNIGHT, SO THEY CALL IT A DAY...

THAT WAS OUTSTANDING!

BUT...

I-35 AND I-240 LOOK COMPLETELY BLOCKED, BUT WE COULD TRY I-44.

LET'S GO FOR IT...WOW, THE AIR SURE SMELLS STRONG TONIGHT.

THAT'S NATURAL GAS AND MASHED-UP VEGETATION – **THE SCENT OF DESTRUCTION.**

THE AREA OF MOORE IN OKLAHOMA CITY HAS BEEN OBLITERATED.

ON I-44...

...WE ARE GETTING REPORTS OF AS MANY AS 40 DEAD AND OVER 500 INJURED...

I LOVE WATCHING THESE STORMS DEVELOP, BUT I WISH THEY DIDN'T GO INTO POPULATED AREAS.

YES, WE SHOULD NEVER FORGET THE HUMAN COST OF THE SPECTACLE.

THE 1999 OKLAHOMA TORNADO OUTBREAK LASTED TWO MORE DAYS AND REMAINS ONE OF THE WORST ON RECORD. **THE END**

TIM SAMARAS
TORNADO CHASER

ELECTRICAL ENGINEER AND VETERAN STORM CHASER TIM SAMARAS HAS DEVELOPED A UNIQUE PROBE DESIGNED TO ACCURATELY RECORD THE ENVIRONMENT *INSIDE* A TWISTER...

...AND SO, THE PROBE'S CONICAL SHAPE MEANS THE WIND FORCES WILL ACTUALLY *KEEP* IT ON THE GROUND.

OUR MAIN PROBLEM IS ACTUALLY **FINDING** A TORNADO TO PLACE THE PROBE IN FRONT OF.

SAMARAS IS BEING INTERVIEWED FOR THE NATIONAL GEOGRAPHIC TV CHANNEL.

TWISTERS ARE VERY RARE EVENTS. DURING THE 2001 AND 2002 SEASONS, WE RACKED UP 50,000 MILES AND DIDN'T SEE A SINGLE ONE!

SO FAR THE 2003 SEASON HASN'T BEEN MUCH BETTER.

ON THEIR LAST FIELD DAY, 24 JUNE 2003, IN SOUTH DAKOTA, SAMARAS AND HIS TEAM FINALLY GET LUCKY...

STORM CENTRE, IT'S A BIG WEDGE, ABOUT HALF A MILE WIDE, ON THE GROUND, HEADED DIRECTLY TOWARD MANCHESTER!

THAT'S A BIG, BIG TORNADO!

FOLLOWING SAMARAS AND HIS CHASE PARTNER, PAT PORTER, ARE GENE RODEN AND PHOTOGRAPHER CARSTEN PETER.

OH MAN, THIS ROAD IS TERRIBLE!

THE TORNADO'S CHANGED TO A CONE SHAPE.

SCREEEECH!

WE'VE HIT ASPHALT, THANK GOODNESS!
TWANNG
CRRACCK
KREEEEECH

AT A SAFE DISTANCE...
DO YOU THINK WE GOT IT?

LATER, AT A MOTEL, SAMARAS DOWNLOADS THE DATA FROM THE PROBE...

OH, BOY, IT RECORDED A PRESSURE DROP OF OVER ONE HUNDRED MILLIBARS WHEN THE VORTEX HIT.

EXTREME!

EXTREME? IT'S LIKE HITTING A BUTTON IN A LIFT AND GOING UP ONE THOUSAND FEET IN TEN SECONDS!

THE WIND SPEED MUST HAVE BEEN OVER 230!

OH, YEAH, WE WERE DEFINITELY TOO CLOSE.

THE END

HOW TO BECOME A STORM CHASER

The pioneers of storm chasing were Americans. The US is still the place to go to hunt storms for a living. In other countries, such as the UK and Australia, storm chasing has become a more popular hobby, with organisations such as TORRO (the Tornado and Storm Research Organisation) whose members exchange information on UK storms and severe weather.

REQUIREMENTS
Knowledge about weather science is essential and storm chasing without this knowledge can be extremely dangerous. You can study for an NVQ in weather observing or a degree in meteorology, oceanography or climatology.

STEPS TO BECOMING A STORM CHASER
1. Take a university degree in meteorology. Many tornado lovers started their chasing days in groups of like-minded students. There are several universities in the UK, such as East Anglia, Reading, Leeds and Liverpool, with good courses in meteorology. If you progress to a Master's degree you might even get a grant to research storms.

2. Train with the Met Office. The Met Office provides training to World Meteorological Organization (WMO) standards or for specialised areas such as aviation and aeronautics. The Met Office employs around 1,800 people around the world although most are at the headquarters in Exeter. Train to be a forecaster, the tornado chaser's 'day job' of choice.

3. Become a Storm Spotter. TORRO is a privately funded voluntary organisation that is supported by a network of observers and investigators (including untrained enthusiasts and experts) who act as its 'eyes on the ground'. Observers report on all types of extreme weather from tornadoes and funnel clouds to hailstorms and ball lightning.

(Main picture) Pilot's-eye view from an NOAA WP-3D Orion as it emerges from the wall cloud of Hurricane Katrina to penetrate the calm of the eye.

The Dimmitt Tornado was photographed as part of Project Vortex in 1995.

GLOSSARY

altitude The vertical distance above sea level.

deploy Launch a probe.

Doppler A type of radar.

eyewall A ring of towering thunderstorms that surround the eye at the centre of a tornado.

forecaster A person who estimates what may happen to the weather in the future.

F scale The Fujita Scale. A way of measuring the power of tornadoes by looking at the amount of ground damage they cause.

funnel cloud A tornado column that narrows as it approaches the ground.

g (pronounced jee) G stands for gravity and is short for g-force.

g-force The force a person feels when accelerating. One g is equal to the force acting on a body while standing on Earth.

landfall The contact of a hurricane with a landmass.

mesocyclone A spinning mass of air around a supercell thunderstorm.

meteorologist A scientist who studies the atmosphere and predicts its weather.

millibars A unit of atmospheric pressure used in meteorology.

mothership A huge storm from which a tornado emerges. The term is derived from the movie, *Close Encounters of the Third Kind*, in which the spaceship is a similar shape to such a storm.

obliterated Totally destroyed.

phenomena Happenings or events, often extraordinary or abnormal.

radar A system for detecting objects in the atmosphere by bouncing electromagnetic waves off them.

reconnaissance Military observation of an area.

rope out To thin out to a rope shape, as a tornado does when it dies.

satellite tornado A smaller tornado that appears near to, and is associated with, a larger one.

storm surge A rise in the sea level, moving forwards in front of a storm, which causes coastal flooding when it hits land.

supercell A severe thunderstorm that can produce tornadoes.

technique Method of carrying out a scientific task.

tornadogenesis The process by which a tornado forms.

translucent Semitransparent – allowing light through only.

tropical Referring to the areas on either side of the equator, between the Tropic of Cancer and the Tropic of Capricorn.

turbulence The irregular movement of the atmosphere.

vortex A whirlwind.

FOR MORE INFORMATION

ORGANISATIONS

Royal Meteorological Society
104 Oxford Road
Reading RG1 7LL
0118 956 8500
Email: info@rmets.rog
Website: http://www.rmets.org

TORRO (Tornado and Storm Research Organisation)
P O Box 972
Thelwall
Warrington, WA4 9DP
07813 075509
Website: http://www.torro.org.uk

FOR FURTHER READING

Allaby, Michael. *Tornadoes: And Other Dramatic Weather Systems* (DK Secret Worlds). London, England: Dorling Kindersley, 2001.

Chambers, Catherine. *Hurricanes* (What on Earth). Brighton, England: Book House, 2006.

Jeffrey, Gary. *Hurricanes* (Graphic Natural Disasters). London, England: Franklin Watts, 2010.

Jeffrey, Gary. *Tornadoes and Superstorms* (Graphic Natural Disasters). London, England: Franklin Watts, 2010.

Orme, David & Helen. *Tornadoes* (What on Earth). Brighton, England: Book House, 2006.

Spilsbury, Louise & Richard. *Terrifying Tornadoes* (Awesome Forces of Nature). Oxford, England: Heinemann, 2004.

INDEX